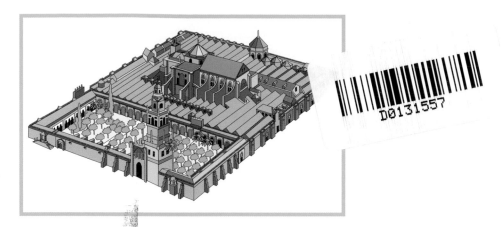

The Mosque-Cathedral of
CORDOBA

Text:
Manuel Nieto Cumplido
Canónigo Archivero de la Catedral de Córdoba

Photographs, design, lay-out and printing completely created
by the technical department of
EDITORIAL FISA ESCUDO DE ORO, S.A.

All rights of reproduction, translation,
either total or partial, are reserved.

Copyright of the present edition covering photographs and text:
© EDITORIAL FISA ESCUDO DE ORO, S.A.
www.eoro.com

⬠ ESCUDO DE ORO

Aerial view of the cathedral-mosque, adjoining which are the labyrinthine streets of the Jewish quarter.

INTRODUCTION

The Islamic section of Cordoba's Mosque-Cathedral is, without a doubt, the starting point for Spain-Moorish architecture on the Iberian Peninsula. It has been said that this is the oldest building, still standing and still in use, in Spain. Its peculiar history –from great Moorish mosque to diocesan cathedral– alone makes it one of the outstanding buildings in the world, and whilst as far back as the 15th century it was claimed to be one of the Wonders of the World, it was finally declared World Patrimony in 1984. An exiled Cordoban of the late-Middle Ages, Jerónimo Sánchez, wrote that the Mosque-Cathedral's beauty made it the glory of Spain, distinctive sign of the honour of Cordoba,

illustrious seat of its bishop and a monument honouring the Christian monarchs buried within its confines.

The Mosque-Cathedral was built on the banks of the Guadalquivir during the period of the Caliphs and originally stood next to the Omeya fortress, flanked by three Moorish baths, one of which, the Santa María Bath, is still partially extant. The whole formed a unique site which the city later took as its seal, along with the main bridge and the Albolafia waterwheel. Though various examples of Renaissance and Baroque architecture (the Puerta del Puente and the Triunfo de San Rafael) have since been interposed, the site can still be admired from the Calahorra Tower on the opposite bank of the river.

The Mosque-Cathedral still forms the vital heart of the Catedral district of the city, containing what was until recently the Bishop's Palace, housed in a former caliph's fortress, now the Diocesan Fine Arts Museum which, enclosed by the original city walls, shelters an 17th century construction boasting a wide Baroque staircase and the Chapel of Nuestra Señora del Pilar, containing altarpieces by the sculptors Pedro Duque Cornejo and Alfonso Gómez de Sandoval. Adjoining is the Conciliary Seminary of

The Chapel of the Virgen de los Faroles and belltower, in the north side of the cathedral-mosque site.

The Patio de los Naranjos.

San Pelagio (18th-19th centuries) with its fine Baroque front. A Roman air is also given to the site in the graceful shape of the Triunfo de San Rafael, a partial replica of the central fountain of Piazza Navona in Rome, constructed in the mid-18th century by the French architect Michel Verdiguier in honour of the guardian archangel of the city.

On the northern side of the Bishop's Palace is what was, up to the 19th century, the Hospital of San Sebastián, and is now the Congress Palace. Outstanding in this building is the spectacular Gothic front of the tiny church, the work of Hernán Ruiz I in the early-16th century. The other buildings surrounding the mosque are houses which, whilst retaining their original design, of Middle Ages origin, are in fact of modern construction.

3

Visigoth altar and Caliphal font.

Door of the extension of Al-Hakam II. ▶

HISTORY

Although historical Moorish sources speak of the existence on this site of a Jewish temple built by King Solomon, reliable historic data begins with the construction of a Christian monastery dedicated to Saint Vincent in the 6th century AD. This was excavated in 1933-35, revealing the foundations of two churches as well as two mosaics. Some of the architectural elements, bases, shafts, capitals and mouldings, are believed to have been used, also, in the Moorish construction.

The building went through two principal historic phases: the Moorish phase, from its construction in the 8th century to the year 1236, and the Christian phase, from 29 June of that year until our times. It was on 29 June 1236 that King Ferdinand, the Holy, on reconquering the city, consecrated the former mosque as a Christian church dedicated to Saint Mary, Mother of God. Its conversion to a cathedral was not marked by any particularly elaborate ceremony as it was the custom in medieval Castile to convert the former mosques of the reconquered towns and cities into Christian places of worship.

What was singular was the admiration for the beauty of its construction shown by those present at that time. Alfonso X, the Wise, wrote that this building, inherited from Islam, surpassed in loveliness and splendour all other Arab mosques, whilst in 1239 archbishop and historian Rodrigo Ximénez de Rada exclaimed that this mosque had no equal in the Muslim world for its ornateness and dimensions. Judgements with which Corbobans, both Muslims and Christians, have been in full agreement throughout its history, without doubt a key factor in the survival of this matchless monument.

The west front of the mosque.

Cathedral belltower (16th-17th centuries). ▶

THE SITE

The site on which the original mosque was erected in the 8th century was, according to the evidence unearthed by archaeologists, already occupied during the times of the Roman empire. The *Via Augusta* which circulated at its foot before crossing the bridge towards Gades (Cadiz) and the statue of Mars and the laurels of Apollo found during excavations in the courtyard seem to bear this theory out. The first buildings recorded, however, are a large constructed site in the 6th century, a monastery dedicated to Saint Vincent and which survived until the year 785, when it was demolished. A wall belonging to this building found under the floor of the courtyard, contains a large number of bricks bearing an inscription proving them to have been made by one Leontino, whose Christian faith is born out by the monogram of Jesus Christ which accompanies the name of the manufacturer. To the west of the monastery was the Palace of Rodrigo,

seat of the Visigoth governors. Moorish sources certify the existence of the Christian church «where God on high was worshipped and the Gostels read». The terms of the treaty of surrender signed on the Moorish conquest of Cordoba in 711 state that the Christians had to give up half of the monastery site, which was immediately dedicated as a mosque by Tariq ben Ziyad, liberto of Musa ben Nusayr. So it remained until the last days of the reign of Emir Abd al-Rahman I who, noting the lack of space to accommodate the faithful for Friday prayers, decided to buy the Christian site. It was precisely in the part dedicated to Islam that the people of Cordoba had sworn allegiance to the first Omeyan emir after the Battle of Al-Musara in 756.

At first, the Christian owners refused to sell, but they eventually yielded to pressure and in 785 Abd al-Rahman paid them one hundred thousand dinars for the site which, once the Church of San Vicente had been demolished, was added to the mosque courtyard.

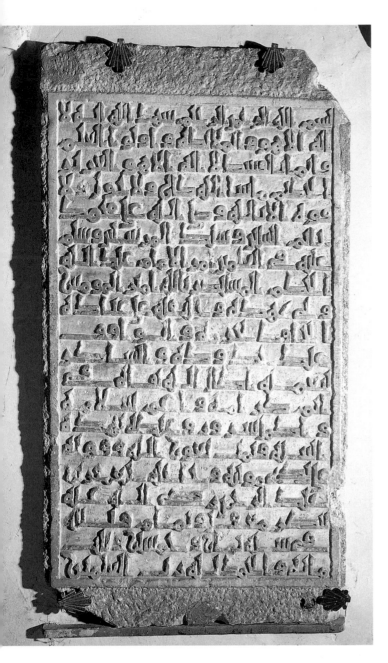

Foundation stone of a building (968).

THE ORIGINAL MOSQUE

In accordance with the agreement reached with the Christians, Abd al-Rahman I ordered the demolition of the church in the year 169 of the Hejira and the construction of the aljama mosque began at the beginning of Rabi I of the year 170, the first days of September in the year 786 according to the Christian calendar.

The feelings of Abd al-Rahman, and perhaps the memory of his Syrian origins, were present from the very start of the work. When the orientation of the new building was being decided, the emir intervened decisively: the mosque was to have the same orientation as the Great Mosque of Damascus in Mecca. Abd al-Rahman, some historians believe, wished to feel himself in Syria when leading prayers as the iman or attending Friday prayers. Though the Abbasi caliphs prevented him from returning to his homeland, Damscus, where his heart lay, could be recreated in Cordoba. Others prefer to believe that the irregular orientation of the mosque was decided by the emir due to his acceptance of the arrangement chosen by the conquerors for the first half of the Basilica of San Vicente, in which the baptistry in the south side was converted into the *mihrab*.

Moorish culture, at the end of the 8th century, was still at an early stage of assimilating the knowledge of other cultures, and the original mosque must therefore be interpreted as the synthesis of what was pre-Islamic Hispanic architecture. It is not surprising, from this point of view, that this mosque has been described at the last Hellenist building in the Western world.

The mosque had an almost perfectly square groundplan, with sides of 79 metres, divided from east to west by a wall into two equal halves used respectively as the courtyard of ablutions and the oratory. The latter space was, in turn, divided into eleven south-facing aisles, perpendicular to the *mihrab* wall or *qibla*. The entrance to the oratory from the courtyard was formed by eleven open arches in the dividing wall, which became in this way the front of the oratory looking over the patio. The crucial invention of the mosque of Cordoba is the use of series of arches made up of columns, pillars, upper round arches and lower horseshoe arche. In order to raise the arches it was usual to supplement the columns with pillars which left arches at the required height, but this structure was very fragile and it was necessary to subject it with strong supports such as were used in El-Aqsa (Jerusalem) and the Qairawan mosque in Tunis. In the Cordoban mosque, the function of these supports is

◄ Abd al-Rahman I arches.
(Pp. 8-9).

Coffering and arches of the central nave. ►
Abd al-Rahman I.

performed by arches, with great benefit to the overall effect and architectural worth of the building. This solution has no precedents and the glory of discovering it lies wholly with the Cordoban constructors. Looking for inspiration, they thought of such Roman aqueducts as that of the Miracles in Merida, with superimposed supporting arches between its pillars (F. Chueca). The formation of the arches, with alternating stone voussoirs and red brick is a construction technique used at the end of the Roman empire. The original mosque in Cordoba had 152 columns with their respective capitals and mouldings, all taken from older buildings. These elements, the serene proportion of the arcades, double in its lower order, and the basilical structure of the building combined to confer on it a Hellenistic air.

The aisles were each covered independently of the others using tiles projecting over the walls of the arcades, where channels were made between the aisles to carry away rainwater.

Such a work of art fully justifies the verses written in honour of the first *omeya* by a poet of the time: *Entregó por Dios y en su honor / ochenta mil piezas de plata y oro / que gastó en una mezquita cuya base es la devoción / y su gloria, la religión del profeta Mahoma. / Se aprecia el oro reluciente en sus techumbres / que brilla con el resplandor del relámpago flameante* (For God and in his honour, he spent 180,000 silver and gold pieces in building a mosque whose base is devotion and whose glory is the religion of the Prophet Mohammed. Gold covers its roof, shining with the splendour of fiery lighting).

Abd al-Rahman I (d. 788) was unable to see the courtyard finished, and it was left to his son and successor, Hisham I, who reigned from 788 to 796, to crown this space with a minaret, high gallery or *sagifa* for women to pray on the north side, and a *mida'a*, or dependency for ritual ablutions, adjoining the outer battlements of the east wall of the oratory, of which the original foundations survive. In 851, Abd al-Rahman III extended this courtyard northwards, built a new, celebrated minaret and reinforced the front of the oratory looking over the courtyard with another adjoining it, with 22 columns supporting its arches.

Wreathed column of Abd al-Rahman I.

Nave of the mihrab, facing the courtyard.

Nave in front of the mihrab.

FIRST EXTENSION

In 832, Abd al-Rahman II ordered two more galleries for the women to pray in to be built on the east and west sides of the courtyard, thus giving this area continuity and harmony. The present porticoed galleries were rebuilt at the beginning of the 16th century and do not correspond to the original arrangement. In 848, Abd al-Rahman II began work on the first southward extension of the oratory, increasing its length by 26.6 metres with the addition of 80 columns, capitals and mouldings, almost all of them open. To these columns must be added the four adorning the *mihrab* and which served as entrance arch jambs, later transferred to the present structure.

These works, directed by the eunuches Nasr and Maswr, were not completed until seven years later, when Muhammed I, son and successor to Abd al-Rahman II, completed the decoration of the new section and restored that of the old. The structure of this first extension was a faithful copy of that of the architects of the preceding century, except for the suppression of the foundation bases. The materials used were also taken from earlier works, but were of a worse quality than those used in the original mosque. The shortage of materials obliged the first Cordoban Moorish capitals to be carved and placed either on nearby columns or on those at the entrance to the second *mihrab*. Some are free copies of classical models, whilst

13

Extension of Abd al-Rahman II.

Dome in front of the mihrab. ▶

others are original creations. It was before this *mihrab* where the *jutba* or solemn sermon was pronounced on 16 January 929 in which the name of Abd al-Rahman II was invoked with the supreme titles of jalifa (caliph) and Amir al-Mu'minin (prince of believers), affirming his absolute territorial and spiritual sovereignty over Moorish Spain.

General view of the second extension of the Mezquita. (pp. 16-17). ▶

Door leading to the Bayt al-Mal or Treasure Chamber.

Mosaics at the Puerta del Sabat or corridor to the Alcázar.

The Mosque: mihrab.

19

◀ *Dome of the mihrab.*

Original mosque with Christian additions.

THE SECOND EXTENSION

On the death of the first caliph in 962, his son and successor Al-Hakam II, a pious prince, ordered a second extension to the oratory, consisting of 45.5 metres of depth on 190 large columns, plus 24 medium-sized columns adjoining the pillars of the *maqsura* and 84 small ones in the domes, making the temple an authentic model of beauty and splendour. The work was carried out with impressive speed, and most of it took just three years to complete. This work of decoration and renovation, adding to the beauty of the mosque, lasted until the death of the caliph.

The same orientation was preserved. Though recognised as erroneous, it was decided to respect the plans of the first architects, whilst to the original mosque were added twelve rows of columns. The support and the sustaining arches repeat the splendid invention of 786. With the exception of the four columns of the jambs of the *mihrab*, transferred from the first extension, all the remaining architectural elements used were made expressly. The columns, alternately of bluish grey and pink marble from Cordoba and Cabra, were adorned with schematically-designed, alternately simple and compound Corinthian capitals, according to the model established by Abd al-Rayhman III for the new front of the oratory over the courtyard, and the bases continued to be suppressed, except in the wall, now perforated, of the second *qibla*.

The Mosque of Al-Hakam II, a monument of Caliphal art, is a veritable model of architectural expression. Its decorative wealth, neither excessive nor oppressive, forms the adornment of a lofty, clear design, its art as mature, refined and exquisite as the caliph who conceived it. What is lost in Hellenism is gained in magical orientalism, with

21

*Entrance
arch to the
Lucernario
of
Al-Hakam II.*

*Interlacing ▶
arches of the
Lucernario
of
Al-Hakam II.*

Nave of Al-Hakam II.

Column in front of the mihrab of Abd al-Rahman II.

Mesopotamic accent, in happy, mysterious contrasts of light and shade (F. Chueca).

Important innovations were also introduced at this stage, the product of the original creations of the Cordoban alarifes, already used in Madinat al Zahra', where important traces still remain: the Oriental-style ornate arches, the crossed arches, the domed pavilions resting on ribbed columns reminiscent of Armenian churches with their double-walled *qibla*, the mosaics at the entrance and the dome of the *mihrab*.

The wealth of the caliphs is concentrated in the decoration of the *maqsura* and the front and interi-

Dome of the Lucernario of Al-Hakam II. ▶

Restored Moorish coffering.

Moorish coffering. ▶

or of the *mihrab*. What most springs to the attention is the profusion of decoration in plaster, except the marble panels flanking the door to the *mihrab*, representing the tree of life, and the sumptuous mosaics on the walls. Attractive floral emblems adorn the alternating red and white voussoirs of the arches and the pendentives, friezes and panels.

At the request of Al-Hakam II, the Byzantine emperor Nicéforo Focas provided materials and artists to decorate the main sections of the building. These Greek artists contributed the mosaics on the horseshoe arches, the *alfiz* (partially restored at the beginning of the 19th century) and the openings of the high arches of the front, as well as the dome crowning this extraordinary space. The decoration is floral for the most part, completed with Cufi inscriptions recalling the work of Al-Hakam with Sura LIX of the Koran. The work was completed with pre-fabricated ceramic pieces placed to adorn the edges of the small tesseras on the mouldings of the dome.

This extension was covered during the same caliph's reign by the addition of a splendid coffered wood ceiling, restored at the beginning of this century, with beams and panels ornamented with fine floral motifs, bows and geometric shapes.

◀ *Arches of Al-Hakam II (pp 26-27).*

Dome of the maqsura.

◀ Dome of the maqsura (pp 30-31).

Arches of the maqsura and front of the mihrab. ▶

Aisle of the extension of Almanzor.

THIRD EXTENSION

In the year 987, the «Almanzor Extension» began, ordered by that ruler during the days of the ill-fated caliph Hisham II. This was the last and most extensive of the three, but did not offer novelties. Perhaps its only original feature is the fact that it occupied the entire east side the length of mosque, to a width of 48 metres, and included the extension of the courtyard with its cistern. Eight new aisles were created, resting on 356 columns, now covered with 18th-century Baroque vaults. It is thought that this extension was merely made for display, no doubt with political aims and to affirm Almanzor's power.

Column and capital of Almanzor.

Altar of Santa Marta.

Door of San Sebastián.

Door of San Miguel.

DOORWAYS AND FRONTS

Of the original mosque only the doors of the west side survive. These are known as the Puerta de los Deanes and the Puerta de San Sebastián (as it opens onto the hospital of the same name). The decoration here, vigourous and perhaps a little excessive, may provide the link between Visigoth and Caliphal ornamentation. The Puerta de San Miguel, altered in the early-16th centu-ry, comprises a lovely blend of Moorish and Late-Gothic art. The other restored doorways of the west side, except the Postigo del Obispo, which again presents a mixture of Gothic and Caliphal art, harmonise the tripartite composition of the Puerta de San Sebastián with the front of the *mihrab*. Almost all the doorways of the east side, by Almanzor, were restored under the direction of Ricardo Velázquez Bosco at the turn of the century.

Palace doorway. ▶

◀ *Puerta de las Palmas.*

Aisle of the Sagrario.

THE CATHEDRAL

The former mosque was consecrated as a Christian church on 29 June 1236 and was converted into a cathedral in 1239 after the ceremony investing its first bishop, Lope de Fitero. At the express desire of King Ferdinand II, the Holy, it was dedicated to Mary, Mother of God, and it became known to priests and laymen alike as the Church of Santa María, and it was not until the 16th century that the cathedral was renamed after Our Lady of the Assumption.

After the consecration and dedication, the first step to convert the former mosque into a cathedral was the closure of the arches opening onto the courtyard, thus desacralising this open space in the same way and form as the cloisters of Spanish cathedrals. Five doorways now communicated the cathedral with the courtyard: two for the cloisters, two for processions in the Sagrario and Santa María del Pilar aisles (closed and walled off since 1973) and that of the former axial nave or *mihrab*, known as the Arch of Bendiciones or Puerta de las Palmas. The main, official, entrance to the cathedral continued to be that of the mosque, now known as the Puerta del Perdón, which opens onto the courtyard and not the interior of the building as in the rest of Hispanic cathedrals. Together with the powerful architecture of the interior, it is this Moorish trait, respected by the Christians, which gives such an exceptional character to this monument.

Chapel of Villaviciosa.

Chapel of Nuestra Señora de Villaviciosa. ▶

CHANCEL, TRANSEPT AND CHOIR

The first chancel and choir were located until the early-17th century in what is now the Villaviciosa Chapel, empty since the late-19th century, when restoration work began in an attempt to restore the building as far as possible to its original form.

The construction of the present chancel and transept, grandiose in form and concept, has been the subject of controversy since work began on them in 1523. The cathedral chapter manifested its opposition to the reforms proposed by Bishop Alonso Manrique (1516-1523) defender and protegé of Emperor Charles V. Just a few days later, the local council announced the death penalty for any builder, mason, carpenter or labourer accepting to work on the demolition of any part of the former mosque, and even before its conclusion, Canon José Aldrete, in name of the bishop and chapter, informed Sixto V that the work had been undertaken with "little prudence".

◀ *Nave of the mihrab (pp. 40-41).*

Side of the transept.

Transept and dome. ▶

1. Architecture and iconography

The aim of the project was to create a vast, airy nave whose interior, simple and without great detail of ornamentation, would produce the effect of the great naves of the Renaissance. The architects were Hernán Ruiz (d.1547), his son Hernán Ruiz II (d.1569), Diego de Praves, who contributed the dome and the vault of the choir, and Juan de Ochoa (d. 1606) who completed the works.

Our attempts to interpret this enormous space, whose walls hamper and diffuse the force of much of the original Moorish building, should not distract us from the concept and understanding of it during the period when the project was being exe-

cuted, or from its medieval Christian liturgical precedents. For example, medieval and 16th-century documentation contains frequent instances when the word «nave» is applied both to the perpendicular aisles of the old *qibla* and the double-arched east-west cross aisles. If not much more powerful, it was at least the vision imposed by the repetition of the series of arches and their spectacular effects. The liturgical east-west orientation, dedicated as far back as the 13th century with the old chancel, only signified with the new chancel the consolidation of one of the two perspectives offered by the building. Moreover, the closer reference to the Hispanic cathedral which, seen in the ground-plan, is greatly similar to the solution suggested by Hernán Ruiz I, was sufficient.

Dome of the transept.

Capilla Real: statue of Saint Ferdinand. ▶

Entrance to the Capilla Real.

Dome of the Capilla Real.

In this construction, according to F. Chueca, successive styles are echoed in layers or strata, similar to the cuttings of geologists in natural terrains. Below is a Gothic-Mudéjar style with a rich Andalusian flavour; next, at the height of the large windows, is a Mannerist layer; and finally, there is the Herreran dome. The least homogeneous element, the choir vault and the wall at its feet, is that carried out by Juan de Ochoa, with one foot in the Renaissance and the other in the Baroque period. The design of this vault is based on the original division into compartments of the Sistine Chapel in Rome.

The iconography of the chancel, transept, choir and side aisles relates to the different stages of the project, the most important of them being the first and third. The stage completed under Bishop Juan Alvarez de Toledo (1523-1537) saw the vault of the ambulatory behind the high altar decorated with illustrations representing the Prophets, Evangelists and the Virtues, as well as the five reliefs in the tympana of the horseshoe arches located in the same space, dedicated to the Passion and Resurrection of Jesus Christ, completed shortly before 1531 by a sculptor whose name has not reached our days.

The vault in the chancel, by Hernán Ruiz II, presents a numerous and important iconography. The central image is the large statue of the Assumption of Mary. Saints, prophets, apostles, angelic musicians and the Emperor Charles form a crown of glory around the figure of the Mother of God.

The choir vault, by the Antequeran worker in stucco, Francisco Gutiérrez, is adorned with the coats

Coro and organs.

Arch adjoining the Capilla Mayor.

Buttress in the coro and Altar of La Concepción.

of arms of Bishop Francisco Reinoso in the central spandrels of the centre and elsewhere, and the figures of David, Solomon, Daniel and Samuel. In the semi-spandrels of the four corners are Faith, Hope, Charity and Strength. In the central band, Our Lady of the Assumption, Saint Victoria and Saint Acisclo, martyrs of Roman times and patron saints of the city, the dome is decorated very much in Counter-reform style: Evangelists and Fathers of the Church as an expression of the Revelation and tradition.

Buttresses at the feet of the coro. ▶

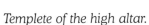

Templete of the high altar.

Statue of Pedro Duque Cornejo in the high altar.

2. Altarpiece over the high altar, pulpits

The construction of this altarpiece is due to the initiative and funding of Bishop Diego de Mardones (1607-1624), whose mausoleum, the work of Juan Sequero de la Matilla, can be seen near the lectern.

On 16 February 1618, the cathedral chapter approved the design presented by the Jesuit Brother Alonso Matías (1580-1626), whose training consisted of study of the treatises of the Italians Vitruvius, Alberti, Palladio and Vignola. Matías proposed that the altarpiece should be in marble and bronze, as this would be cheaper, there being abundant marble available in the nearby quarries at Cabra, Luque and Carcabuey. However, in 1625, by order of the General Father of the Company of Jesus, Brother Matías was forced

to abandon this work and the post of Cathedral master builder, though not before he had written an extensive description of the design to be followed. The work was taken over, first by Juan de Aranda Salazar (1627-1629) and later by the Portuguese artist Juan Vidal (1629-1652), who respected the plans of Brother Matías. The great sculptures adorning the altarpiece are by Pedro Freile Guevara and Matías Conrado, whilst the bronzes are the work of Pedro and Diego de León, Antonio de Alcántara, Pedro de Bares (d. 1649) and Juan Redondo. Alonso de Mena carved the Agnus Dei for the custodia (now in the Seminary of San Pelagio) in 1646. The paintings representing Saint Acisclo and Saint Victoria,

Vault of the high altar. ▶

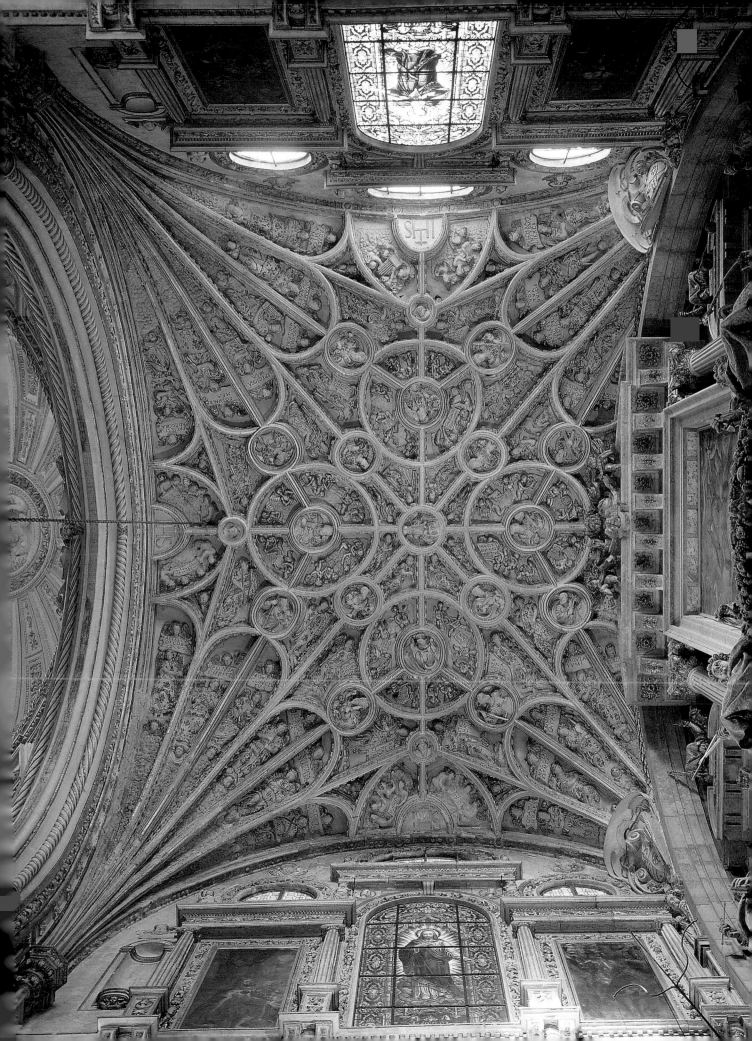

Presbytery: statue of Saint James.

Tomb of Bishop Diego de Mardonos.

Saint Pelagio and Saint Digna, Cordoban martyrs from Roman and Moorish times, and the huge painting of the Assumption, are by Acisclo Antonio Palomino in 1714.

This altarpiece, according to M.A. Raya, was conceived within a unique, monumental order in which the outstanding features are the verticality of its panelling, achieved through the use of a single axis uniting the two bodies, giving it a Baroque air.

The altarpiece stands over an altar table in silver, the donation of Bishop Pedro Antonio de Trevilla in 1818, designed by the chief architect of Madrid, Manuel de la Peña Padura. Also remarkable is the large silver lamp, donated by Bishop Cristóbal de Lovera and the work of Martín Sánchez de la Cruz (1629).

The pulpits, the idea of Bishop Martín de Barcia (1756-1771), were constructed over the period 1762-1779, and are attributed to Miguel Verdiguier of Marseilles (d. 1796), who is also thought to have done, at least, the symbols of the Evangelists on which the pulpits rest, whilst the medallions of these are attributed to Alfonso Gómez de Sandoval.

The iconography of the medallions is adapted to the liturgical act of each of the pulpit. Those on the Epistle side depict scenes from the preachings and pastoral activities of the Apostles, whilst those on the side of the Evangel feature scenes from the life of Jesus.

Coro and high altar. ▶

Pulpit on the side of the Evangel.

Pulpit on the side of the Epistle.

Symbols of Saint Matthew and Saint Mark.

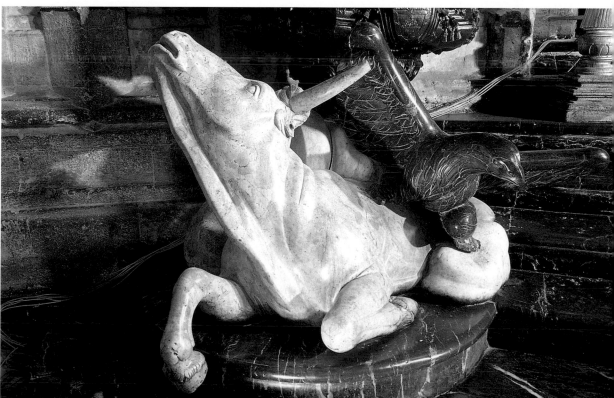

Symbols of Saint Luke and Saint John.

Chapel of San Bernabé.

Gothic reliefs behind the high altar. ▶

High altar:
Relief of the
Passion.

High altar:
Relief of the
Resurrection.

High altar:
Relief of the
Passion.

High altar:
Relief of the
Passion.

◀ *High altar:*
Relief of the
Passion.

◀ *Painting of*
Our Lady of
Carmen and
reliquary.

Marble
altarpiece in
the Chapel
of La
Presentación.

Baptismal
font (1723).

Choirstalls and altarpiece in the Capilla Mayor.

Choirstalls and bishop's throne (coro). ▶

3. Choir stalls

The construction of these splendid stalls in mahogany from the Antilles began in 1742, when the chapter received a generous donation for the purpose. After long deliberations and study of various designs, that of Pedro Duque Cornejo, now buried at the entrance to the choir, was chosen. Pedro Duque Cornejo began work in 1747 and declared the stalls complete in 1757, the year of his death at the age of 80.

The bishop's throne, conceived as an altarpiece, crowns the entire choir. Its decorative elements are completely due to the personal devotion of Bishop Miguel Vicente Cebrián of Saragossa (d. 1752), which explains why the medallion of the bishopry bears the image of the Apparition of the Virgin of the Pillar to Saint James. The medallions on either side this depict Saint Vincent Ferrer and Saint Michael, after whom the bishop was named, Saint Joseph and Saint Anthony of Padua. Flanking the scene depicting the Ascension are statues of Mary Magdalene and Saint Theresa, and the entire scene is crowned by a statue of Saint Raphael, patron saint of the city.

According to R. Taylor, the choir stalls are an unusual work for their time, not just for the richness of the materials used, but also for their design and arrangement. The decoration includes scenes from the main Old and New Testament stories, making the stalls a modern *Biblia pauperum*. The presence of depictions of the

Detail of the choirstalls.

Lecturn in the coro.

Cordoban martyrs on the lower stalls represented, without doubt, an attempt to theologically link the diocesan church with the entire story of the Saviour.

The work is completed by the figures of the four Evangelists in the four corners of the choir and two 18th-century English pendulum clocks.

An exception piece, formerly in the old choir, is the cast brass lectern in the form of eagle, from a workshop in Malinas (Netherlands) and dating back to the early-16th century. At its foot are the figures of the Virgin with Child, Saint Catherine and Saint Barbara.

Coronation of the Bishop's throne in the coro. ▶

Organ on the side of the Evangel.

Organ on the side of the Evangel, above the coro. ▶

4. The organs

That on the Evangel side was constructed during the bishopry of Don Francisco de Alarcón (1658-1675), whose escutcheon it bears. The Valencian organ-makers Miguel and Bernabé Llop signed the contract for the construction of this organ on 17 March 1666. The work was completed in 1671. The box was made by Bartolomé Mendigutia, son of the then master craftsman of cathedral. It was consists of six bellows, two manuals, an entire wind chest with 56 grooves and various registers. It was restored almost completely reconstructed by the Cordoban organ-maker Patricio Furriel over a ten-year period, then again at the end of the 19th century by the Belgian maestro Ghys, and finally restored and electrified by Organería Española in 1957-1960. Patricio Furriel also built the organ on the side of the Epistle. The Neo-Classical box is decorated by a painting of Saint Cecilia by Diego Monroy Aguilera, crowned by a sculpture of the Archangel Gabriel. So painstaking was the work of Furriel that from a hired builder he and his team of assistants passed to become salaried cathedral employees. The wind chest was completed in 1827.

In 1892, this organ was found to be in a very poor state of repair by Bishop Sebastián Herrero (1883-1898), who paid for its restoration, also carried out by Ghys. The organ consists of the following reeds: *trompeta real* (royal trumpet), 26 flute, 13 flute, octave, violin, octave flute clarinet, bass, *orlo*, counterbass, *pajaritos*, *campanillas*, royal clarin, bell clarin, trumpet, fifteenth, *gamba*, voix céleste, harmonic flute, clarinet and vox humana.

The Cathedral chapter recently commissioned Federico Ocitoris of Torquemada (Palencia) with the restoration of both organs, and work is expected to be concluded in 1996.

Portapaces of Bishop Fernández de Angulo.

TREASURE, OR CATHEDRAL MUSEUM

This is housed in the Chapel of Santa Teresa, also known as the Chapel of Cardenal Salazar, and in the two rooms in the old *sabat* or gallery behind the *qibla*. The idea of creating a museum to exhibit the treasure was first ~~muted~~ suggested by González Francés at a chapter session on 18 March 1896.

The pieces exhibited are all objects pertaining to the activities cathedral, except for a number of items used by the chapter (desks) or the bishop (staffs, pectoral crosses, rings, etc). The 473 pieces exhibited were donated by bishops, canons and laymen or purchased.

From the 16th to the 19th century, the cathedral always had its master silversmith. Some of the most brilliant of these were Rodrigo de León (c. 1539-1609), Pedro Sánchez de Luque (1616-1641), Bernabé García de los Reyes (1725-1752) and Damián de Castro (1752-1793).

The most singular exhibit in the museum is the processional custodia. The cathedral chapter commissioned the German silversmith known as Enrique de Arfe, born in Harff near Cologne in 1514, with its construction. It is possible that the commission was impulsed by Archdeacon Francisco de Simancas (d. 1520), a devotee of the Eucharist, who donated all his silver for the work. Chapter records testify that Enrique de Arfe had already begun work on 7 September

Processional monstrance by Enrique de Arfe.

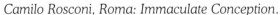

Camilo Rosconi, Roma: Immaculate Conception.

Statue of Our Lady, by Damián de Castro.

1514, and the custodia was first used in the Corpus Christi procession of 1 June 1518. The custodia is 262 cm high, whilst its base measures 92 cm.

The work has three sections resting on a decagonal base with various levels and great decorative wealth. The lower level was added in 1734-35 by Bernabé García de los Reyes so as to increase its height. The outer faces depict the groups who danced in the 18th century procession: carriage, dance of the choirboys, groups of men and of women. The base also contains three inscriptions recording the main restoration dates, 1735, 1784 and 1967.

This 18th-century base supports the other levels making up the basement, separated by crenel-lations. The last level of the basement contains 18 niches with fine reliefs in silver depicting scenes from the Life of Christ.

Resting on this splendid basement is the first body, covered by an ovolo dome under which is the portable custodia, whose foot is from the second half of the 16th century. It is supported by a hexagonal socle decorated with the Tree of Jesus.

The second section is the kiosk containing the silver statue of the Assumption of Our Lady, by Bernabé García de los Reyes. Its dome is perforated and over it rises the architectural structure of the third section, crowned by an ovoid piece adorned with emeralds, serving as the base for the Resuscitated.

Holy Thursday Urn, by Damián de Castro.

Chalice of Archbishop Delgado Venegas.

Reliquary of Saint Bartholemew.

The museum also contains the following outstanding works:
- 13th-century rock crystal processional cross.
- Archdeacon Simancas' processional cross in silver gilt (c 1515) by Enrique de Arfe.
- Bishop Mardones' processional cross in silver gilt (1620) by Pedro Sánchez de Luque.
- Silver sceptre of Bishop Diego de Alava, by Rodrigo de León (1561-1562).
- Silver sacra of Bishop Cebrián. Early-17th century.
- Sacras of Bishop Barcia, made in Rome. 1756-1761.
- Lecterns of Racionero Murillo. Silver-plated. By Pedro Sánchez de Luque.

- Silver gilt portapaces of Bishop Fernández de Angulo, by Pedro Fernández (1515).
- Silver gilt portapaz of the Adoration of the Magi (1530).
- Portapaces of the Marquis of Comares, by Rodrigo de León (1578).
- Easter Thursday Arc of teh Eucharistic by Damián de Castro, 1761.
- Statue of Our Lady by Damián de Castro, 1757 (silver gilt and colour).
- Statue of Saint Raphael by Damián de Castro, 1768 (silver gilt and colour).
- Reliquary of Saint Stephen, 1398-1426. Gilt silver.
- Reliquary of Saint Bartholomew, mid-15th century, with rock crystal chalice.

*Cross of
Bishop
Mardones.*

Rodrigo de León: stoup of Bishop Alava.

Monstrance of Las Cuarenta Horas.

Pedro de ▶ Córdoba: Annunciation.

Treasure: ivory crucifix.

Damián de Castro: Saint Raphael.

pedro de cordova pintor

esta obra e rretablo mando fazer diego sanches de castro canonigo desta iglia a onrr de dios nro señor e de su santa incarnacion ciclos bij· armirados
sa sua bupta e santiago e sa llorente e sato ju de bretaña e de sato pio papa eu santa barbara/acabose a x x· dias de março año d jv·mil·lxxv· años

Coronation of the Chapel of La Concepción.

Chapel of San Simón y San Judas: Statue of the Nazarene.

CHAPELS

The chapels, for the most part adjoining the perimeter walls are arranged as in most cathedrals. The two easternmost and westernmost aisles have been closed off since as far back as the 13th century, as has the former *maqsura* adjoining the south wall. This space was originally created for the mausoleum of the founder and his descendants and family, and alms were offered here for their souls.

1. Chapels of the west wall

There are ten chapels to be visited on this side, dedicated from north to south to: Saint Salvador and Saint Ambrose (fine Baroque altarpiece by Teo-dosio Sánchez de Rueda in 1723); Saint Augustine and Saint Eulalia, founded in 1409 and containing a large painting of Saint Raphael in his apparition to P. Roelas, by Antonio Alvarez Torrado in 1788; and Saint Simon and Saint Judas, consecrated in 1401 and adorned with a Baroque altarpiece featuring the haut relief of Jesus of Nazareth (16th century).

The Chapel of Nuestra Señora de la Concepción occupies what in the *Middle Ages* was the baptistry. It was founded in its present state by Bishop Fray Alonso de Medina y Salizanes as the bishops' mausoleum. Work began in 1679, and the chapel was

Altarpiece of the Chapel of La Concepción. ▶

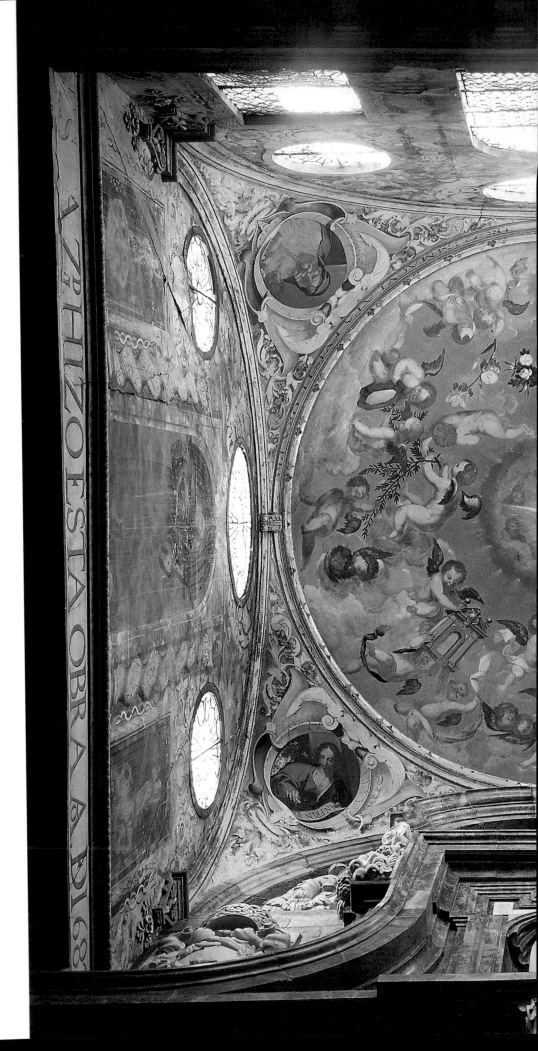

Dome of the Antechapel of
La Concepción.

Chapel of San Antón: statue of the saint.

inaugurated on 2 December 1682, its construction causing alterations to the outer section of the west wall.

The antechapel is covered with a media naranja decorated by paintings attributed to Juan de Alfaro, with images of saints Mary and Francis. The entrance is formed by a doorway in red marble from Cabra and a grille by Pedro de León (1682). The richly-decorated interior features an altarpiece by Melchor de Aguirre and statues by Pedro de Mena. On the sides are the praying figures of Saint Ildephonse of Toledo and Bishop Alonso de Salizanes.

Next is the Chapel of San Antón or Antonio Abad, which contains a statue of the saint in the niche of a Baroque altarpiece dating back to the late-17th century. The Chapel of the Santísima Trinidad was founded in 1401, but the stucco altarpiece with painting of the Trinity, by the Catalan artist José Saló, dates back to 1864. Next, to the south, is the Chapel of San Acasio y Once Mil Vírgenes, founded by Bishop Fernando González Deza (1398-1424), which was completely restored and reorganised in the early-18th century. Cupola and altarpiece are by the sculptor Teodosio Sánchez de Rueda (1714), who was hired by contract to restore an *Ecce Homo*, to sculpt a statue of Saint Acasio and to paint seven canvases by the Italian artist known here as Juan Pompeyo.

Lastly, is the part-Mudéjar (1399) Chapel of San Pedro y San Lorenzo, which dates back originally to the 13th century, though its present ornamentation is from the 18th century. The altarpiece features an oil on canvas painting of Saint Peter curing the paralytic, an Italian copy of the original by Cigoli (1605-1621). Outside, on the south wall, is a large canvas of the Last Supper by Pablo de Céspedes, painted between 1593 and 1595, after the artist's second visit to Rome. Technically, he is said to have imitated the beautiful manner of Antonio Correggio, one of the greatest of the Spanish Colourist painters. The frame is by Juan de Ortuño in 1595.

Chapel of La Santísima Trinidad.

Blind door in the Chapel of San Pedro. ▶

Detail of the Altarpiece of San Acacio.

2. Chapels on the south wall

The Chapel of San Esteban y San Bartolomé has the added value of being the final resting place of Luis de Góngora (d. 1627), in a burial urn designed by Carlos Luca de Tena and made at the workshop of the marble cutter García Rueda with adornment by the silversmith F. Diaz Roncero. It was founded in the 13th century, but its link with the Góngoras can only be traced back as far as the second half of the 15th century. The Baroque altar-piece-frame features a painting of the martyr Saint Bartholomew, a modest copy by a local master on

Chapel of San Acacio: Ecce Homo.

84

an engraving by José de Ribera (1626). The tiles on the table date back to the late-15th century.

The Chapel of Santa Teresa, or of Cardenal Salazar (1630-1706) was originally designated the main sacristy of the cathedral, just as it had been the sacristy of the mosque, which explains the presence here of various liturgical objects and ornaments. Its construction was designed and directed by Francisco Hurtado Izquierdo (1669-1725). The plasterwork of the cupola are the work of Teodosio Sánchez de Rueda in 1702. In 1712, Teodosio Sánchez de Rueda was commissioned to undertake two exhuberantly-carved frames for the paintings of the Conception and the Assumption, attributed to Juan Pompeyo. Under the sacristy, with the same groundplan, is the crypt containing altarpieces and paintings by Juan Pompeyo.

Between the arches of the chapel, on niches, are statutes of saints, carved, like that of Saint Theresa, by José de Mora. The stucco altarpiece was made in 1798 and may be attributed to Ignacio de Tomás. The three large canvases representing Saint Ferdinand, saints Acisclo and Victoria and the Apparition of Saint Raphael to P. Roelas respectively were painted in 1713 by Acisclo Antonio Palomino.

The Chapel of San Inés, founded in 1350-1363, is adorned with a lovely marble and stucco altarpiece by the French artist Baltasar Dreveton (1761) The statue of the saint is by another French sculptor, Miguel Verdiguier.

At the side, to the east, is the Altar of La Encarnación, featuring a splendid panel by Pedro de Córdoba (1475) and depicting the Annunciation. At

Juan Pompeyo: Immaculate Conception (Chapel of Santa Teresa).

Chapel of Santa Teresa: statue of the Assumption.

Tiles on the Altar of San Bartolomé.

the foot of the Virgin is Saint John the Baptist and Canon Juan Muñoz, Saint James and the second founder, Diego Sánchez de Castro, Saint Lawrence, Saint Pious I, Saint Ibo of Brittany and Saint Barbera.

In the southwest angle is the former Chapel of Santiago, since 1571 dedicated as the parish church of the cathedral. Its interior is completely decorated with frescoes by the Italian artist Cesare Arbasia (1547-1607). The head of the central nave depicts the Last Supper, whilst the side altars feature two canvases by the same author. The remaining decoration features Roman and Cordoban Mozarab martyrs. Its organisation is based on the *Uomini famosi*. In the lunette over each group of martyrs is a landscape painting, a field of art in which Arbasio reached great fame.

The gilded polychrome wood carving of the Tabernacle is by Guillermo de Orta, a Flemish sculptor (1578). The gilding and quilting is by Alonso de Ribera.

Chapel of La Asunción: relief of the altarpiece.

Tomb of Cardinal Salazar. ▶

S. AVGVSTINO

SRAMON NONTO

Altarpiece of the Chapel of San José.

Statue in the Former Chapel of La Concepción.

3. Chapels along the east wall

The first is the Chapel of La Asunción de Nuestra Señora and is ornamented by an altarpiece designed by Hernán Ruiz II in 1552 and made by the sculptor Juan de Castillejo. The panel paintings were recently attributed to Pedro Fernández Guijalvo. The splendid grille bears the date 1554.

Next is the Chapel of la Natividad de Nuestra Señora, with altarpiece by Martín de la Torre (1567) and large painting of the Generation of Mary, by Gabriel Rosales (1578). Next, to the north, is the Chapel of San José, founded in 1349. The Baroque altarpiece, dating back to around

◀ *Last Supper, by Pablo de Céspedes.*

1720, features a 16th-century carving of Christ on the Column.

The Chapel of Nuestra Señora de la Concepción was founded in 1379. It features a Mannerist altarpiece by an anonymous artist. The paintings on the bench are by Miguel Ruiz de Espinosa (1547), as is the carving of Saint Zoilo.

Adjoining is the Chapel of the Espíritu Santo, founded in 1568 by the Simancas brothers, two other bishops of Ciudad Rodrigo and Cartagena de Indias respectively. The paintings are by Hernán Ruiz II (d. 1569) and his son, Hernán Ruiz III, who completed the work. Purist Andalusian themes are handled in miniature, but with such an intensity as to become Arabesques.

The Chapel of Nuestra Señora de la O or Expectación was founded in 1364. The altar-

Altarpiece of Santa María de Guadalupe.

Altarpiece in the Chapel of La Limpia Concepción.

piece dates back to 1743 and the painting of the Annunciation is by Pedro Moreno in the same year.

The Chapel of San Nicolás de Bari was founded in 1262. Francisco de Castillejo was commissioned to gild, paint and quilt the altarpiece, according to the directions of Hernán Ruiz II, in 1556. The statue of Saint Nicholas is by Francisco Martínez (1549). The altarpiece was wholly remodelled in 1623. The panels were painted by Pedro de Campaña, a Flemish painter, in 1556. On the Evangel side is an altarpiece dedicated to Our Lady of Guadalupe by Francisco Ruiz Paniagua (1679).

Next is the Baptistry, transferred here in 1679. The al fresco altarpiece on the south wall was painted by

Pedro Moreno in 1723. The iconographic programme and verses on this painted altarpiece are by P. Juan de Santiago, S. J. The bluish-grey jasper font dates back to the same period, its interior of alabaster and the lid carved and gilt.

The Chapel of San Juan Baptista was founded in 1260 by the First Lord of Aguilar. It contains a fine altarpiece, designed, no doubt, under the watchful gaze of Hernán Ruiz III, with a structure after Palladian canons. It was reformed with a Baroque touch by Manuel Molero Cañas de Oro in 1720. The paintings are thought to date back to the last quarter of the 16th century, though their author is not known.

The Chapel of La Limpia Concepción, whose closure is believed to have been supervised by Hernán

Ruiz III and carried out by Cristóbal Guerra (d. 1574), contains an altarpiece by Francisco de Vera (1581). The paintings are by Baltasar del Aquila (1582-1587). The lovely tiled frontal depicting the story of the Good Samaritan dates back to the same period.

The creation of the Chapel of Santa Ana was charged to Juan de Ochoa in 1596, and is the first with walls and iron gate. The paintings adorning the altarpiece have been attributed to Pablo de Céspedes and A. A. Palomino.

The Chapel of San Antonio de Padua is the last chapel on the east side. It was constructed by Sebastián Vidal, whose mortal remains are buried at the entrance. The altarpiece is dedicated to the same master. The paintings are attributed to the Cordoban artist Antonio Fernández de Castro Villavicencio (1659-1739).

4. Chapels on the north side

Among these, outstanding is the Chapel of the Benditas Animas de Purgatorio, founded by the Inca Garcilaso de Vega in 1612. The statue of Christ Crucified is by Felipe Vázquez de Ureta. Also interesting are the Chapel of Nuestra Señora del Rosario, with paintings by Antonio del Castillo (1647); that of Santo Cristo del Cautivo or of La Uña, whose existence is testified to by records dating to as far back as the year 1581; and those of Los Santos Reyes, San Miguel, Nuestra Señora de la Antigua, Santa María Magdalena, San Esteban and San Eulogio.

Detail of the Altarpiece of San Juan Bautista.

Chapel of San Antonio: statue of the saint.

BIBLIOGRAPHY

AGUILAR PRIEGO, «Datos inéditos sobre la restauración del Mihrab de la Mezquita de Córdoba», Brac, 54 (1945), 139-166.

ALCOLEA, S., Guías Artísticas de España: Córdoba, Barcelona, 1963.

BRISCH, K., «Las celosías de las fachadas de la Gran Mezquita de Córdoba», Al-Andalus, XXVI (1961) 398-426.

CAMPS CAZORLA, E., Módulo, proporciones y composición en la arquitectura califal cordobesa, Madrid, 1953.

CAPITEL, A., «La Catedral de Córdoba. Transformación cristiana de la Mezquita», Arquitectura, 256 (1985), 37-46.

CASTEJON, R., La Mezquita Aljama de Córdoba, León, 1971.

CRESWELL, K.A.C., Early Muslim architecture, 1979.

CHUECA GOITIA, F., La Mezquita de Córdoba, Granada, 1968.

GOLVIN, L., Eassi sur l'architecture religieuse musulmane, 4, L'art hispano-musulman, París, 1979.

GOMEZ MORENO, M., «La civilización árabe y sus monumentos en España», Arquitectura, II (1919) 310.

HERNANDEZ GIMENEZ, F., «Arte musulmán: La techumbre de la Gran Mezquita de Córdoba», Archivo Español de Arte y Arqueología, XII (1928) 191-225.

HERNANDEZ GIMENEZ, F., El alminar de Abd al-Rahman III en la Mezquita de Córdoba, Granada, 1975.

MARQUEZ, C., Capiteles romanos de Corduba Colonia Patricia, Córdoba, 1993.

MARTIN RIBES, J., Sillería del Coro de la Catedral de Córdoba, Córdoba, 1981.

NIETO CUMPLIDO, M. - LUCA DE TENA, C., La Mezquita de Córdoba: planos y dibujos, Córdoba, 1992.

NIETO CUMPLIDO, M., La miniatura en la Catedral de Córdoba, Córdoba, 1973.

OCAÑA JIMENEZ, M., «La Basílica de San Vicente y la Gran Mezquita de Córdoba», Al-Andalus, VII (1942), 1-20.

OCAÑA JIMENEZ, M., «Arquitectos y mano de obra en la consturcción de la Gran Mezquita de Córdoba», BRAC, 102 (1981) 97-137.

RAYA, M. A., Catálogo de las pinturas de la Catedral de Córdoba, Córdoba, 1988.

RUIZ CABRERO, G., «Dieciseis proyectos de Velázquez Bosco». Arquitectura, 256 (1985), 47-56.

STERN, H., Les mosaiques de la Grand Mosquée de Cordoue, Berlín, 1976.

TAILOR, R., El entallador e imaginero sevillano Pedro Duque Cornejo (1678-1757), Madrid, 1982.

TORRES BALBAS, L., «Las tres primeras etapas constructivas de la Mezquita de Córdoba», Al-Andalus, III (1935), 139-43.

TORRES BALBAS, L., Arte Hispanomusulmán hasta la caida del califato de Córdoba, Historiador de España de R. Menéndez Pidal, V, 1957.

PLAN OF THE MOSQUE OF CORDOBA

1. Puerta del Perdón.
2. Postigo de la Leche.
3. Puerta de los Deanes.
4. Puerta de San Esteban.
5. Puerta de San Miguel.
6. Postigo de Palacio.
7. Postigo del Sagrario.
8. Puerta de Santa Catalina.
9. Puerta de las Palmas.
10. Courtyard of the Oranges.
11. Cloister.
12. Aisles of Abderramán I.
13. Extension of Abderramán II.
14. Extension of Al-Hakam II.
15. Aisles of Almanzor.
16. Capilla Mayor.
17. Transept.
18. Pulpits.
19. Choir.
20. Chapel of Villaviciosa.
21. Capilla Real.
22. Chapel of San Pablo.
23. Mihrab.
24. Chapel of Santa Teresa and Treasure.
25. Last Supper.
26. Visigoth Museum of San Vicente.

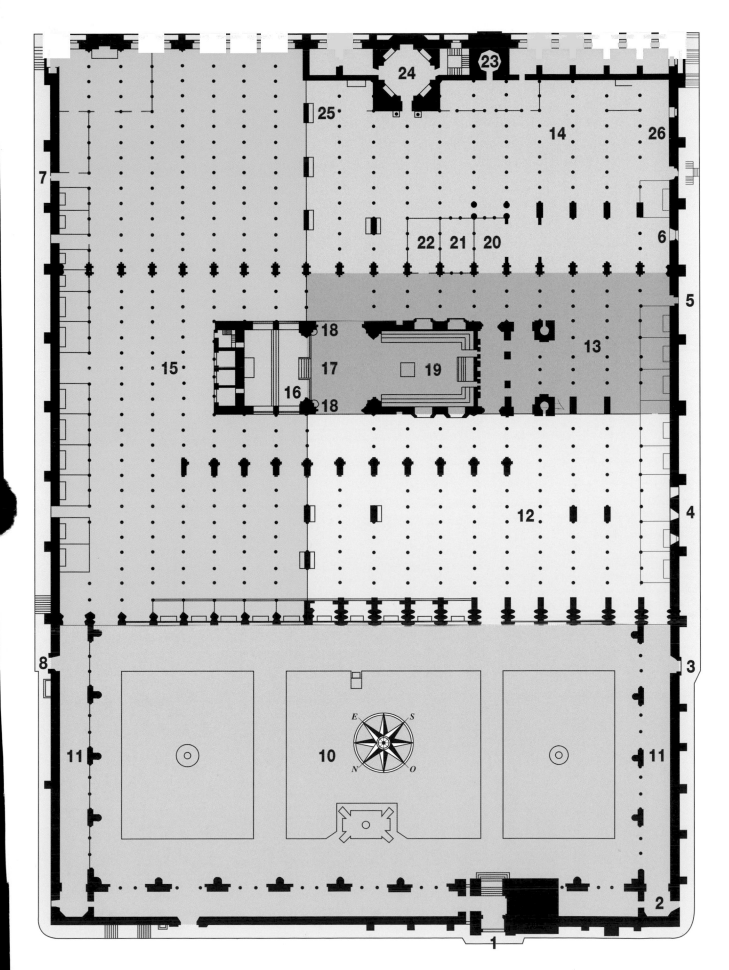

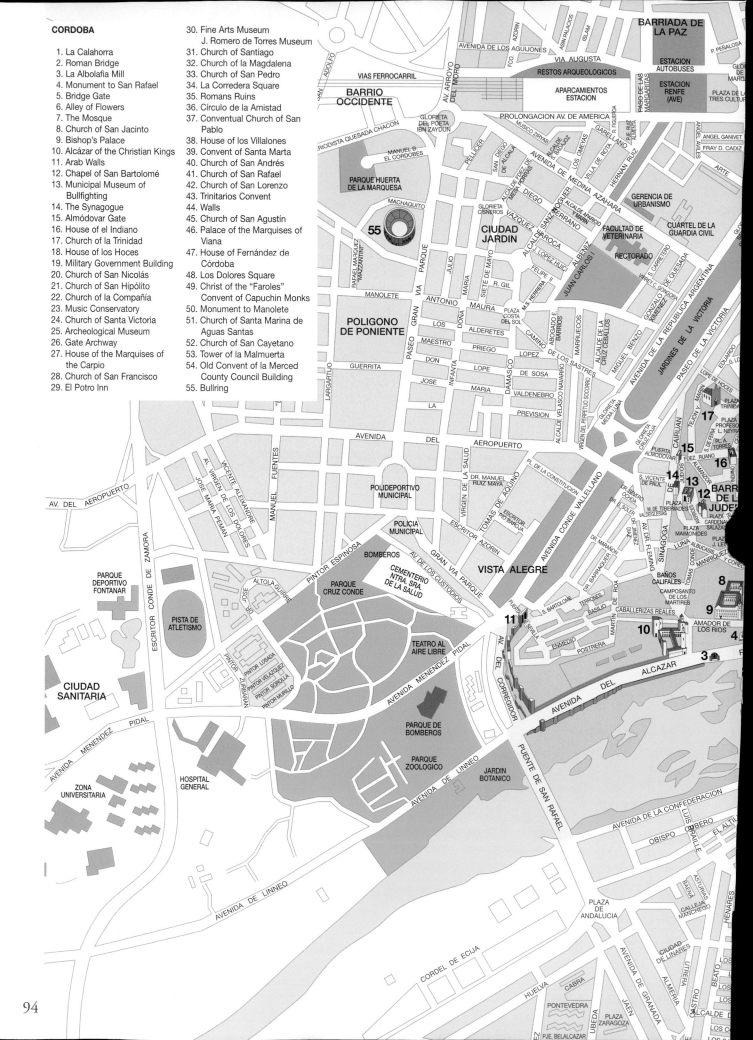

CORDOBA

1. La Calahorra
2. Roman Bridge
3. La Albolafia Mill
4. Monument to San Rafael
5. Bridge Gate
6. Alley of Flowers
7. The Mosque
8. Church of San Jacinto
9. Bishop's Palace
10. Alcázar of the Christian Kings
11. Arab Walls
12. Chapel of San Bartolomé
13. Municipal Museum of Bullfighting
14. The Synagogue
15. Almódovar Gate
16. House of el Indiano
17. Church of la Trinidad
18. House of los Hoces
19. Military Government Building
20. Church of San Nicolás
21. Church of San Hipólito
22. Church of la Compañía
23. Music Conservatory
24. Church of Santa Victoria
25. Archeological Museum
26. Gate Archway
27. House of the Marquises of the Carpio
28. Church of San Francisco
29. El Potro Inn
30. Fine Arts Museum
    J. Romero de Torres Museum
31. Church of Santiago
32. Church of la Magdalena
33. Church of San Pedro
34. La Corredera Square
35. Romans Ruins
36. Círculo de la Amistad
37. Conventual Church of San Pablo
38. House of los Villalones
39. Convent of Santa Marta
40. Church of San Andrés
41. Church of San Rafael
42. Church of San Lorenzo
43. Trinitarios Convent
44. Walls
45. Church of San Agustín
46. Palace of the Marquises of Viana
47. House of Fernández de Córdoba
48. Los Dolores Square
49. Christ of the "Faroles"
    Convent of Capuchin Monks
50. Monument to Manolete
51. Church of Santa Marina de Aguas Santas
52. Church of San Cayetano
53. Tower of la Malmuerta
54. Old Convent of la Merced
    County Council Building
55. Bullring

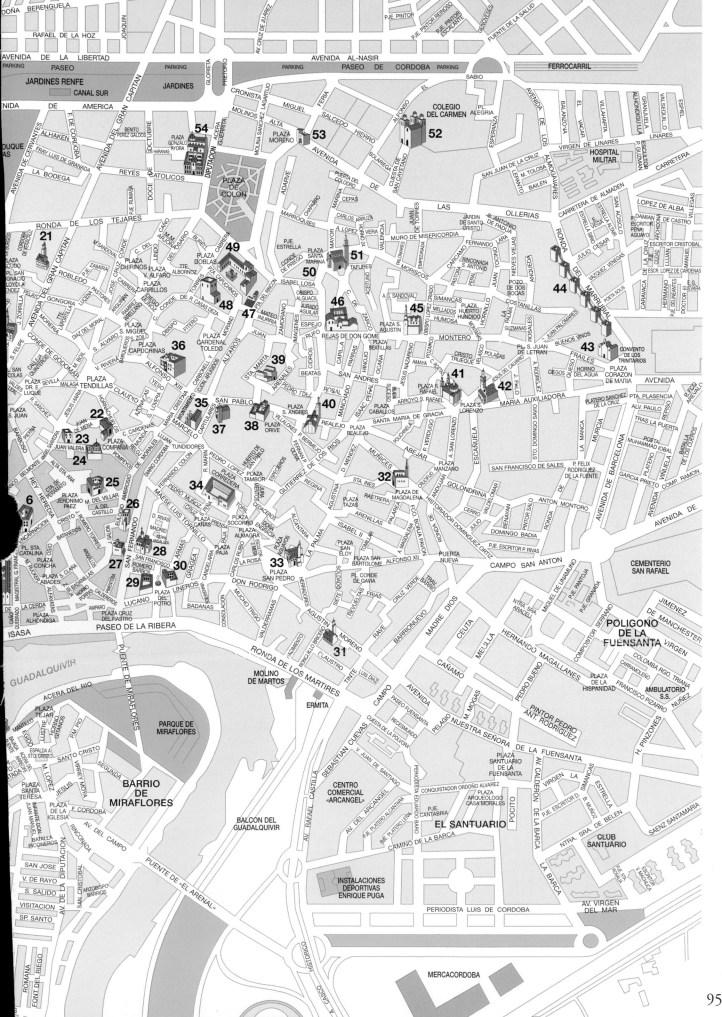

CONTENTS

I.S.B.N. 978-84-378-1673-9
Printed by FISA - Escudo de Oro, S.A.
Legal Dep. B. 864-2007

Protegemos el bosque; papel procedente de cultivos forestales controlados
Wir schützen den Wald. Papier aus kontrollierten Forsten.
We protect our forests. The paper used comes from controlled forestry plantations
Nous sauvegardons la forêt: papier provenant de cultures forestières controlées